Bright Side of the Pale Moon

By

Esha Montgomery

Dedication

This book is dedicated to the dreamers that still believe. I am so proud of this book and I am thankful for all the love I received during its creation and inception. I immediately knew that I wanted this book to be personal. I wanted to draw a story or better yet a whole world with my words and I feel that I achieved just that. Throughout this whole process, I was stressed out while writing but God kept me. This year has been wild like straight up insane. I would say the equivalent of a fish living on dry land type of crazy but if you search you can always find the bright side of the pale moon. This book is for you.

Love always, Esha

Table of Contents

Prologue

A soft rose petal will be my resting post. I'd rather lie on the concrete than not go for broke. Wear wooden earrings, drink vanilla flavored java and act woke. That ain't me... I'm here to give the people what they need. We all need quotes and anecdotes that run deep. Like lost boats formerly seeking passage now sunken to the bottom of the sea. Some allow the truth to rest in peace. That ain't me. I'm digging to break through to a bigger reality. Sometimes people wonder what I'm doing this for. I want the world and my family to read the sentiments from the heart of a word wielding warrior.

-Esha

Part 1

When you fight fire with fire it is nearly impossible to win without watching everything you created burn.

All I Have

I don't have much to give outside of poetry. Sometimes, I don't really think one person can even make a difference! But I pray now more than ever that my words are able to give someone in the world solace. If I can just make one person laugh, smile or think then that's good enough for me. And one day those same sentiments will come along to uplift me too.

Hope's Song

Hope sings a lullaby to me
On feathered wings high above the ground
It flies with no ceilings
But when it comes down

I receive a gift or two
Some old desires brought into view
And a new dream to hold onto
You would be amazed
By what hope can do

On days when it drizzles
And I can't see the sun through the clouds
Those moments when my heart drops
And rain drenches my confused brow

I will still sing
By directing my attention to grander things
Like a duck shaking off water from the stream
One bad day isn't enough to stop me
I pick up my staff like Moses and part the sea
I am beloved by the King of Kings
Angels sings a lullaby to me on feathered wings

Pink Elephant

Beat the drums with loud anxious palms
We tap codes that only heaven knows:

Let the barren sky accept our smoke signals from the crackling fire
Let the world see our destress
Let the mountains tremble with fury
Let the air ascend to heights
So high that it touches God's nostrils

He will smell the scorched earth
And see the blackened sky
Send a downpour O Lord
To wash away our suffering
Send an eagle with sharp talons
And a keen eye to lead us home

Send silver and gold
For the blood that we have given
And the seeds that we have sown

For the land our ancestors tilled

From sun up to sun down but never owned
For the sharecroppers that migrated
To northern fields
For the scars at the cusp of my great
Grandmother's breast that never healed

We became the nightmare that the world hated
But no one ever asked how we feel
We are all connected
To the pink elephant in the room
That no one wants to acknowledge as real

Need Rest

Close your fatigued, heavy eyelids
Let the troubles of yesterday
And fretting over the things
You failed to say
Droop and drift away...

Now take a deep breathe
Accept what is and what will be
By releasing your stress
Everyone has their own path to tranquility
But we all need rest

Cold Wind

How do we begin to process hurt?
After losing the conditions of everyday normalcy
This has become my phantom limb
We fight to reconcile changes

That our hearts have yet
To acknowledge in full stride
We fondle with cobweb covered memories
Connected to rust colored fantasies
That are taken by the tide

Its arrival marked the first winter's snow
The truth stings like a cold wind's blow
We hustle to the warming centers
To stop our dreams from getting frostbite
Try as we can, pray as we might

Monologue: Trying to Convince

The space that exists between us is deafening to me. It tears away at my shallow, poorly constructed endeavor to build a relationship with you worth fighting for. I scream at you when you're not around, uttering words behind your wide back. I call you everything but a child of God in my mind because I fail to properly love you or myself. So I push off my inconsistencies and narrow in on yours. A child on a fool's errand. But beneath the earth's surface, at the crater of my origin story, lies my bruised and fragile soul begging for you to accept me. So I can begin the process of accepting myself. I guess I've been waiting all my life. Counting the seconds, hours, days, weeks that it will take for our not so different paths to cross again.

A Prayer

You can do it, you always do it
I act like I'm fine but you see through it
Lose a job, lose a man
Got no plan but I'm not foolish

Cuz you give clues to the clueless
You are the guide for the lost
A healer for the ailing
A tutor to the failing
A coach for those who lack ambition
A roadmap for the clergy on a mission

You paid rent when my account was below
Spared me from eviction
When my former colleagues said,
A single women with no man
And no revenue couldn't keep a home

You held my mother down and lifted her up
When the doctors told us it was time to give up
You made the impossible feasible
When hope was in short supply

Now in my hour of need
I look toward the rainbow in the sky
Lord afford me the grace to overcome
The tangled web of contoured innervation
That haunts the solace in me

Cuz you give clues to the clueless
You are the guide for the lost
The healer for the ailing
I am a caged bird in the midst of breaking free
Please nurture my soul and give me relief

Shallow Mistakes

Who am I to judge, what I don't understand?
I see you doing wrong
But fail to realize…
Where the complications all began
God has your role established in a larger plan

While I am consumed
By an ever-growing ignorance
Assuming I know your past and present
But never cared to give you a chance
As time goes on and you share with me
I realize that my knowledge of you and myself is incomplete

How can I touch your heart?
When I failed to meet you where you are...
To put it plain and simple... I can't
For years you were abandoned

And needed someone in your corner
But was consistently treated like a hooligan
I know that sorry won't cut it.... but I am
With newfound hope, I pray we can start again

You can spend your whole life knowing someone...
But never understand what their going through
When all is said and done I want you to know

That despite my imperfections... I love you

Not Giving Up

I don't got much to give
In this late night session
But I'm gonna turn a little into a lot
Add water to the juice I brought

Shake it up and keep it moving
One foot in front of the other
The right never questioning
What the left is doing

Keeping to the pace of the horizon's music
Casting off doubters, their hate is foolish
We live among zombies, the walking ruthless
When your stomach is knocking on rock bottom...

It's hard to make legitimate excuses
It's downright useless
Get it legally or parlay with streets that leave dragons toothless
But we press on...

Knowing the struggle won't last forever
And a brighter day is coming along
As long as you give your goals fuel and stay strong!

Look out into the ominous crowd

I bet you see a detractor
Someone who compared your genius to the mad hatter
Talk about a social disaster

What people called you
In the past, present and future doesn't matter
They knew you had dreams
So they set fire to your ladder

Figured you wouldn't be able to get to the top
With no stair master
But not giving up
Means you look for new answers

Precarious Love

What is it?
This delectable love thing...
Is it teeth clenched (on an ear pull)?
Or is it the air pushed off a bat's wing?

We don't know what it is
But it awakens every sensation in the body
It goes on dates
It lives to party

But oddly...
It fails to deliberate
Easily turning into silent jealousy and open hate
An invisible line which seals love's fate

One day it was wickedly toxic
The next... it's beyond great
We dance on the winding spindle of give and take
Never willing to give up (until it's too late).

What is it?
This delectable love thing...
It is teeth clenched (on an ear pull)?
Or is it the air pushed off a bat's wing?
Foregoing the origin
It has been known to make a numb heart sing.

Awake

The trust is eroded
I've given up on everythang
That I latched on too
Bet you didn't notice
Never thought I would separate from you

So your binoculars lost focus
But just like the ocean
I waddled away feeling blue
Once I was taken in by your glow

Now it's hard to think the way I use to
While being pushed away
By a force I never knew
And at the core of it all...
Is the fear that I still need you?
Is the desire that I still want you?

Is the reality that I can't continue?
To lie in bed at night with both eyes open
Waiting for a breakthrough
Big enough to shake you... awake

Starting Over

The struggle of starting over again
Lies in the process...
Create it:

Piece by piece,
Layer by layer,
Inch by inch
You mold its form.

Use the love embedded
In your open palms
To keep it warm.

Then embellish it
With each morsel of your reverie
That was torn.
Voila! A new opportunity is born

A Dawn Not Yet Risen

There is no magic just dust
Noise halts to nothingness
And blank stares follow
The sidewalks once full are hollow

I hear tire screeches...
Cars stopping, bodies dropping, babies crying
All in the pale desolate twilight
Of a dawn not yet risen

You don't gotta sell them drugs
To make a living!
Connect with the plug
And market the turmoil he's bringing
Don't fall for it!
The wise know the sound of the streets calling
But we ignore it!

Manipulating those in the trenches
Won't sustain your life
What you know about an honest day's work
And the midnight grind?

There is no magic just dust
Noise halts to nothingness
And blank stares follow
The sidewalks once full are hollow
Because bullets ain't got no name

We lost one too many to the game
And *the end* is an unknown time...
But because we both live in this neighborhood
Your fate is intertwined with mine
So when you're out here conducting business
Keep the people it affects in mind

What is Dark?

Is it the color we see when the lights go out?

Or is it just a different spectrum of light?

Is it associated with the trepidation?

Of the boogeyman gaining lethal power at night?

Why are people intimidated by dark hues?

Ignoring their function in everyday news

But they love utilizing coal,

Fuel their cars with oil

And wear onyx to embellish jewelry

Spar to retain the strength of obsidian might!

Bypass the pupil's blackness that permits sight

But we raise hell

When our eyes are not working right

A raven swoops down

To the dusty, ground floor

Chirping in a dismal tone, "*use me no more*"

Pour out a forty ounce on a freshly painted ebon street

It matters not... how much you drink

The sun bakes fresh concrete

Like the chocolate chips in decadent cookies

What is dark?

Is it the color we see when the lights go out?
Or is it just a different spectrum of light?
Is it associated with the trepidation?
Of the boogeyman gaining lethal power at night?

The mind fully charges in the twilight
When the predators hunt
And sleep is embraced by the prey
When the shadows chase bodies at play

Ascending owls colliding with bats
And a talking wind
Not heard during the day
Blackness implanted into a world
Growing as complex as the Milky Way

Fury

My fury is bright like a blinding white
It washes out everything in sight
It is the sun...
Bowing to no man but shining for everyone

You want to stare at it
But it burns too hot
Boiling coffee straight from the pot
Onto a flat tongue

The smell of magnolia's float
In the steady breeze
Their petals are caught
In the branches of wise trees
The bees go into frenzy

My fury is tight like spandex pants
The night of thanksgiving
Never tired and always willing to relax

My Fury is bright like a blinding light
It washes out everything in sight
It is the sun...
Bowing to no man but shining for everyone

Random notes make their way from incoherent throats
Startling alley cats, rats and squirrels passing by

Like swirling mist enhanced by the night life

My fury likes to get high
It's the sun touching down
In the afternoon sky

Part 2

Sometimes there is no safe place... So we must look for comfort in the eye of the storm.

What Is Grace?

It's the power to walk away from a bad situation with your head held high. The courage to take the high road even when it adds on additional travel time. Or maybe, it's the way you make people feel when you leave. The twinkle in your eye as you turn your head and wave goodbye... ever so delicately. You send people sailing on smooth accolades when you talk subtly about life. It's the efforts you take to do what's right. You are the bee's knees because you live with grace and you walk with ease. In times like these, we need people who stand above their enemies.

Ills of Man

I can't be angry at you anymore
Tying myself and my heart in knots
Tripping over my own legs following after you
Has left me feeling discombobulated

We are separated by mindset
I could put your progress in an Easy-bake oven
10 years of baking
And you still ain't rise none

Because you're light has dimmed
It has sunken like the Titanic
To a depth that only the Atlantic Ocean knows
Dismissed beginnings covered by hatred's sea

Is my skin color offensive to thee?
I pity those who fail to recognize good company
But as a child it use to get to me
I use to feel upset

When a white kid named nick
Use to call me nigger...
Whenever, I swung on the swing
I would yell with glee
While he spouted obscenities

The racism his parents taught to him

Was disappointing to me
Why fill a child's head with prejudice and bigotry?
While I matured, he remains frozen
In the vestiges of playground stories

That I told to my school friends
Where his connection ended with me
Is where my growth began
It takes strength to stand above the ills of man

As a child, I decided not to take
Other people's problems personal again
A liar is gonna lie
And a sinner has got to sin

Rare Gold

It may glisten in the light
And be a sight to behold
They offer it to you
As though it is better off sold
But beware my love
All that glitters is rarely gold

Survival of Essence

I see through to your soul
Reaching over ruined, decayed rhetoric
And broken concrete roads
To a paradise long departed
But a frankness that the downtrodden proletariat know

Battered pants tattered
And full of holes like the 80's
Yellowed teeth with thick plaque
Covering the surface of eroding enamel
Trailed by ferocious dragon breath

Hands covered in peeling skin
Equivalent to shedding scales
Sunshine eyes with darkened diamond pupils
Cloaked in sadness and horror

Claw your way out of the paper bag
Suffocating the depth of your desires
Believe in more, elevate higher
Keep your existence alive
By adding logs to the crackling fire

I see the pain in the arch of your torn soul
When you limp through the streets
Of unkind parishioners speaking of righteousness

But casting cold blooded, stale sentiments
Of icy discord onto sore wounds

I see through to your soul
Reaching over ruined decayed rhetoric
And broken concrete roads
To a paradise long departed
But a frankness that the downtrodden proletariat know

Continue to hold your head up high
Let your inner power
Desecrate the arrows of the enemy
Created by the plight
Of a cruel capitalistic society

That thrives on the maintenance of your hurt
But no matter the condition of the struggle
Put the survival of essence first

The Stairs

The luminous glow of breaking sunshine
Is dimmed in the hallway
Leading up to my salvation
The shadows of past footsteps...

Lay in the steep darkness of flashing bulbs
Dwindling to a close offset by a backdrop
Of chestnut wooden planks leading down
Urge me to keep inching forward

Sweat drips from a brow unmaintained
By a damping cloth
It flows like hot maple syrup
Between my supple breast

I look down at the power
Which carries me upward and onward?
The legs which grew apart
Were brought together
By a trek intent on pushing togetherness

The steps seem to last forever....
I grip the side-rails for support
But my hand slides ever so slightly
And I slip out of balance with my stride
But I keep walking toward the light anyway

My calves are stronger than they were
yesterday

I curve my attention
When fatigue creeps in-between
The creases of my thighs
Just as my spirits rise
My eyes fell on the stairs
With polarizing singularity

Missing Pay

Get to it
Business in need of getting done

Cheers to the midday
Drinking to shake the pain away

Checks short from missing overtime
And lack of pay

But you still go to work:
Monday through Friday

A Dream in the Pasture

Fighting in your sleep last night
Left raccoon eyes coated in red
A swaying yet diligent, bobbing head
Moves to dreamless cloud shaped melodies

Beyond you lies lavish emerald colored grass
As far as the eye can see
In the day, it calls for you at work
Beckoning you to rest in deep ZZZzzz.....

Customer's words framed by rapid incoherence
blow past
Like the echoing laughter from a love
That penetrated time but failed to last
The ground falls beneath wobbling feet

While your balance is predicated
By the counting of sheep
As you search in a pasture
For the staff of Little Bo-Peep
May it lead you home to opulent sleep?

In God We Trust

We have been here before
We know the color of dusk

The day waits for you
The evening stands beside us

Believing in a God
That few chose to trust

Rhythm of Life

When I was but a child
Every year, before the first frost
Turned moving vitality into hibernating stillness
I would watch all the ducks fly away

I can still recall asking my Mother,
Where are the birds going?
She smiled into my eyes and said,
Their going south for the winter

I couldn't help but wonder how the birds knew
About the season changing
With no weatherman
But every year just like clockwork they left

Until...one fall,
I noticed the ducks weren't flying away
For warmer climate anymore

Confusion set in and I went to my Mother
And said, *Why haven't the birds flown away*?
With a stern look in her eye,
She replied, *The land owners clipped their wings... Now their unable to fly*

Within less than 3 years,
I watched their population dwindle and die

Perpetrators diminished their chances of survival

Failed to care about the rhythm of life

Water Pressure

When the water stops flowing, we look to the pipes. Wondering if the corrosion has obstructed its accessibility? Only to realize that the bill far exceeds the water pressure and our paycheck fails to cover the balance due. Without running water God is the only one I turn to. My dry lips hunger for water but my soul is thirsty for the Lord. His name will unleash blessings so that my cup may be filled to overflow once more.

The Soup Simmers

In my house robe with my bonnet on
While cooking dinner...
I try to see past the hate
The lies and painful reality on my TV

A squeeze of lemon,
A hint of lime,
A dash of salt, heated by a flame
Over 4 minutes of precious time

The sharpened daggers in clear blue eyes
The desperate screams and foregone cries
Buried beneath American fantastical
That burns a whole in my withering soul

As I fight back tears
And the Black Death that has taken hold
The tales of two cities has peaked
There is an internal reckoning

Taking place in a country divided
Those not affected
Or distraught by systemic oppression…
Deny it!
But the soup continues to simmer

A squeeze of lemon,
A hint of lime,

A dash of salt, heated by a flame
Over 4 minutes of precious time

Next Door

I am easy to talk to
But hard to reach
That's why me and my neighbors
Don't speak

We flow through the motions
Of symmetry
For sake of looking good
People in need of a friendly face
In the hood

So we grin
Never knowing intent
Just know that when hell fire blow
I can't come to you to vent

If shit hit the fan
And I can't pay my rent
I'll be on a different block
Fake smiling again

Does it matter?
What order it's in
If it feels right
Looking for acceptance
Under florescent light

The mood calls for

Self-indulgent pleasure
But the mind encourages
The pursuant of a better life
So while Chicago is sleeping
The entrepreneur is awake at night

Moths crowd the broom closet
A swing and they take to the floor
Eating away at the material
Your body once adored

I am easy to talk to
But hard to reach
That's why me and my neighbors
Don't speak

Vintage

Pick it up off the floor
Dust it off
Can it be resurrected?
Its beauty restored

Does it hold true in fluorescent light?
Is the foundation strong?
Things that hold their value are worth the time
So polish it, repaint it
And find a way for its presence to be utilized

Some stuff you throw away
But vintage pieces can be revitalized
You can only realize what you have
By opening your eyes

Not So Long Ago

Tucked in between the pages of history books
And my 84 year old cousin's memory nooks
I found a home:

A haven for Black owned businesses
And a plethora of two parent homes
Set against a backdrop of…
You got this Sista, keep pushing forward
From your Brotha in arms

A protector that keeps known and unknown
Black women safe from harm
Riding up North to city life
Theys migrating to better things

Making a way to break free from the tyranny
Of everyday living under systematic oppression
Buried deep in my Grandma's memory
Carried in my Father's eyes
Lies freedom from modern day slavery

With every breath of my love:
I hear shackles break
I hear worlds collide
I hear an angel's trumpet
Breaking through clear blue sky

Ushering me to give life a try

While the past beckons me
To push forward to a new home…
Where I can lay my Black feet down to rest
Worry no more, fear no more
But live with love forever

Heavy

Another one gone, 3 shakes to the wind
Glistening, listening wanderer
It will take you under
Then bring you up again

No one searches for him
Cuz they know where he be
DANGER – high voltage
Stay off the streets!
You may think you're up to something big
But you'll still get beat

He addicted to the hustling
He love the grind
Running from death in overtime
But this ain't new

And what the hustle did to your friends…
May be done to you!
When things are upside down
Who do you turn to?

Another one gone, 3 shakes to the wind
Glistening, listening wanderer
It will take you under
Then bring you up again
So don't be so naïve

Dealing, stealing and robbing comes in 3's
Keep that shit away from your family
Cuz the blood soaked truth
Waters concrete weeds

No Guidance

With mournful eyes...
We watch society crumble and fall;
The blind leading the blind
To nowhere at all

Talk

Brotha can we talk?

No fists, no knives, no guns and no baseball bats

There is a time and a place for physical combat

But the youth need to see

How level headed adults negotiate

We must unify like flocks of birds

Taken to the baby blue sky

There can be no pride in just getting by

Stronghold Before Me

I called out to him
Like I had done...
So many times before
Only to get
Silence in response

He is distant
With no interest in drawing close
Protected by an impregnable fortress
That remains well guarded

Inside the courtyard,
German Shepherds with teeth
Like sharpened knives
Are on watch...
Your small forces
Send flying boulders to halt trespassers

Electric fences that leave
Scorched earth jealous
Wrap around the castle
Like a parent hugging their child
On the first day of school

A hand dug moat
With a channel too small for a ship
And water too stagnant to sail a boat
Lies before my feet

Why you gotta be so mean?
You’re using archers
To shoot arrows from angles
That I can't see
Let your drawbridge down and face me

Part 3

Love is like grains of sand running through nimble, oily fingers. It's hard to hold on to but you try to grasp it anyway.

Choose You

Misery is always in need of friends to abuse. Toxic connections that consistently share bad news. No attention paid to the hearts broken and emotions misused. Never let someone else's shortcomings give you the blues. Sometimes walking away leads to a breakthrough. Always be ready to choose you!!!

Thunder

He runs with the deadly, sublime thunder
Burning through misty fixed air with predestined might
Loving the look
And the howling sound of rolling light

He curtails his body to its quick movement
Blending into the explosive glow against the expansive night
Never knowing where he will end up
But always ready for another fight

Passionate fury strikes
Ripping through calm sky
Like a thin veil stretched too tight
But he's only human
So his endurance is tapped sometimes

An electrifying dose of power energized a cunning mind
A feeble body is left working in overtime
Nevertheless... when the shock dips down under
He runs with the deadly thunder

L Words

Love and lust
Both start with L's
But they’re nothing alike
It’s the equivalent
Of comparing day to night

Better You

I won't wait for the better you
To arrive
I will take you as is...
The truth suits you

No tailor could ever sew stitches so exact
It matches your delicate frame
You struck a matchstick
Against the sandpaper of my pain

In the trenches of the deep
My anger is being numbed by poetry
And their agony calls your name
But all the same…
I won't want/ nor wait for the better you

Tedious

Your hands have studied my body
Over a thousand times
But every week...
They find something new
I'm infatuated with the tedious nature of you

Fake Apologies

I am a jilted lover
On the break of insanity
I brake fast
And reach for my humanity

He spins tales
Like charlotte is his mother
He go missing
Like a distant brother

He tells me to calm down
When his warm air... tempted the waters
He covers himself in that alabaster oil
But his actions are ungodly
It's hard to accept fake apologies

We Interlock

It's 6:40 am, you call me, and I wake up
Brush my pearly whites, swiftly shower,
Get dressed, put on my makeup

And take notice of the fading shadows outside
Dash out the front door into the unknown abyss
I look back one last time
As I hop into your ride

I cast my mahogany glare
On your countenance and we fall...
Into an ever engulfing robust reality:
Where beanstalks grow in place of trees
And progressing leads you to climb
In search of everlasting green

We interlock our fingers
Like woven braids
We interlock our lips
When we misbehave

We interlock our hearts
When we're feeling brave
We interlock our mission
To reach far goals

Understanding that God
Comes before silver and gold

Eventually we bare our pointed fangs
And our anxious, weary souls

As we drive onto the highway
Headed towards domestic life
Grits, toast, eggs
And disagreements free of strife

We nap in a little slice of paradise…
Nestled in the serenity of our tone
Where eternal love is your guide
And higher creativity encourages
Ambitious souls to roam

Togetherness

We are made for each other

Like peanut butter and jelly on buttered toast

Wind blowing through the sails of a wooden boat

A nonprofit with a mission predicated on hope

Two star crossed lovers that dare to elope

This may be a trilogy in the making

We are connected like a foot to pavement

We fall like the burning ash being knocked off a cigar

We got that comb to kitchen kind of attraction

Whenever you press heat to a greased mane

You get a reaction

Like opposing magnets attaching

Togetherness makes the impossible happen

Vine Love

My weak stomach turns sour
At the taste of rotten grapes
Devoid of their youth
But in 10 years' time...

Bad fruit turns into aged wine.
It makes a cold night warm
And a hot day fine
My love grows on a spiraling vine.

No Longer Hidden

Silky hands talk steady
To permeable marble skin
Quiet thoughts are exchanged
In focused glances
Between determined lovers
As passion rose in the dim candle light

It twirled with the aroma of sweet incense
The sound of the rain fall became our radio
The tapping of the headboard
Will be our Morse code
We spoke louder...

Then the open fire crackled
And its light glistened
Against our bare sweaty bodies
No longer will we hide...
From each other or ourselves

Swift love

Shorty got a scrapbook
In his bedroom
With pictures of me
And what we use to be in it

Letters once sealed
By a lipstick kiss are smudged
Into the depth of eternity
Hushed conversations shared between us

In a lush forest
With fingers intertwined
And feet parallel to mine
Like wild horse murals

Frozen in the springtime
Swift love once ran our hidden utopia
We were outliers
Living on the fringe
Of our own desires

But no more…
The owl hoots
On the arch above our door
The dream's end wraps around us

Like creeping plants
Searching for warmth

After being tasked to live
With no sunlight

Frozen in the springtime
Swift love once ran our hidden utopia
We were outliers
Living on the fringe
Of our own desires

Yesterday's Seeds

Pull back the heavy curtains
On this whimsical narrative
We were forged
In the fire of humble beginnings
Determined to thrive

We make sense
Out of a penny's worth
Of knowledge of logic
We plant seasoned seashells
In barren gardens

Then pray for cold, adequate rain
Pray for strength on weak days
And the ability to sustain
While enduring toil and pain

We watch little seeds
Turn into blossoming plants
That yield food worthy
Of our living room dinner plates

We take comfort in knowing
More than we did yesterday

Call Me Sunshine

I am a chocolate sunrise floating over still land
A part of God's divine plan
People regard me as beautiful
But fail to understand...
That my existence is not equated
To the abundance of man

Pull out your paint brush and stroke...
The deep, broad curves
Of my burgeoning, candescent silhouette
People may think they have seen
The last of my bright rays
But they ain't seen nothing yet

I will levitate above doubt come morning
While the pale moon puts snoring minds to bed
I am the first light you see
When you lift your head
Some call me Sunshine.

Can't Buy

Free forming locks
Twisted into ecstasy
And thrown in a bun
You look good for yourself
Never needing the approval of anyone

360 waves
And a low fade
Poetic justice box style
And micro braids

Afros dancing in a zephyr
Lace fronts riding high
With hair so long
Its touching thigh

Kinky curls getting searched
At the airport to get a mile high
To think they call it the friendly skies
Just remember you have the flavor

That retail can't buy
You stand before a full audience
In limbo
They want to clap
But need a reason for applause
You grin nervously

The butterflies in your stomach
Flutter around in need of acceptance
They pulsate when you grin
When you're nervous they spin
And fly in unison
Looking for a way to break free
Praying for a safe place to be

In this uncertain space you are fully aware
That's it now or never
Do or dare
To fight against the power of anonymity
And let your voice ring out in the solemn air

There is now intensity to your walk

A supernatural component lies in your stare
Only the swelling of butterflies
And a bottle of tequila could bring you here
Blissfully astute but artistry unaware
Open to the possibilities but shut off to care

Sound is more than noise; it's a place, a feeling, a reason to be...

Sound Type

What does your sound feel like?
Is it bass pounding?
Strong enough to shake walls
Is your crescendo fast?
Or does it stall and build up climatic walls?

Is it delicate like wind chimes?
Blowing in the southern breeze?
Or does it float easy like autumn leaves?
Does it dance around the room?
Like cigarette smoke in a hookah lounge

Can it recognize trespassing?
Or does it ignore caution and break pass
The barriers formulated to destroy freedom?
Does your music creep up on the audience?
Like a burglar walking on their tiptoes?

Does it smell sweet like a boutique of roses?
Underneath unsuspecting noses?
Or does it take flight
Like a jet racing down an airstrip
Ascending to the sky
What does your sound feel like?

Till Next Time

This book would not have been possible without the readers and dynamic daydreamers that push my imagination to new heights. Your kind sentiments and support became my fountain from which all inspiration flows. I thank God for your presence in my life.

Love always,

Esha

www.ingramcontent.com/pod-product-compliance
Lightning Source LLC
LaVergne TN
LVHW020657100826
845148LV00012B/2536

* 9 7 8 1 7 3 6 6 5 8 5 0 5 *